Eleanor ROOSEVELT

Eleanor ROOSEVELT

Mary Winget

Lerner Publications Company
Minneapolis

To Mom, Dad, Audrey, Bryan, Nan, and Chip

A special thanks to my son, Bryan, for technical assistance and to my editor, Sara Saetre, for her guidance

A&E and **BIOGRAPHY** are trademarks of the A&E Television Networks, registered in the United States and other countries.

Some of the people profiled in this series have also been featured in A&E's acclaimed BIOGRAPHY series, which is available on videocassette from A&E Home Video. Call 1-800-423-1212 to order.

Lerner Publications Company
A division of Lerner Publishing Group
241 First Avenue North
Minneapolis, MN 55401 U.S.A.

Website address: www.lernerbooks.com

Library of Congress Cataloging-in-Publication Data

Winget, Mary.
    Eleanor Roosevelt / by Mary Winget.
        p.   cm. — (A&E biography)
    Includes bibliographical references and index.
    Summary: Discusses the personal and public life of the woman who was First Lady during the difficult years between the Depression and World War II.
    ISBN 0-8225-4985-9 (lib. bdg. : alk. paper)
    1. Roosevelt, Eleanor, 1884–1962 Juvenile literature. 2. Presidents' spouses—United States Biography Juvenile literature. [1. Roosevelt, Eleanor, 1884–1962. 2. First ladies. 3. Women Biography.] I. Title.
II. Series.
E807.1.R48W474 2001
973.917'092—dc21
    [B]   99-32497

Manufactured in the United States of America
1 2 3 4 5 6 – JR – 06 05 04 03 02 01

CONTENTS

Eleanor Roosevelt toured the South Pacific in 1943 as a representative of the Red Cross. Here she greets sailors on an aircraft carrier.

Chapter ONE

ELEANOR

THE YOUNG SAILOR LOOKED AS THOUGH HE COULD hardly believe his eyes. He was lying in a military hospital bed more than 20,000 miles from home. The battles of World War II (1939–1945) were being waged all around him in the South Pacific. Yet leaning over him was Eleanor Roosevelt, the First Lady of the United States. Dressed in a neat Red Cross uniform—an international symbol of hope—Eleanor was smiling gently, offering words of comfort.

In 1943 Eleanor Roosevelt traveled 23,000 miles in an unheated military plane that took her to Australia, New Zealand, and seventeen other South Pacific islands. Included in the 44 pounds of luggage she was allotted was her portable typewriter.

The important generals and admirals in the South Pacific had dreaded Eleanor's coming. She was, after all, the wife of President Franklin Delano Roosevelt, and they didn't welcome taking responsibility for her safety.

They tried, at first, to limit her visit to the safest places. They surrounded her with military police and high-ranking officers everywhere she went. But Eleanor hadn't come all that way to be shielded from the war by generals and admirals. She had come to see the troops.

In the military camps where Eleanor stayed, she awoke each day at reveille and had breakfast with the enlisted men. She rode hundreds of miles in open jeeps to visit soldiers in far-flung encampments. She warmly encouraged troops about to be sent into battle. She visited hospital after hospital. She walked down every hallway, stopped into every ward, and shook hands with every wounded soldier. Often she attended receptions in the evening, but she never went to sleep without writing her four-hundred-word newspaper column, "My Day."

Eleanor's presence on the front lines often created quite a sensation. After one three-hour flight in the middle of the night, Eleanor landed on the airfield at Guadalcanal. Some trucks loaded with servicemen were arriving too, so she waved. One young man shouted, "Gosh, there's Eleanor!"

Eleanor's energy astounded many people. Admiral

William F. Halsey was one of the people who had advised against Eleanor's visit. He began to change his mind, however, when he watched her in action. "I marveled at her hardihood, both physical and mental," he said. "She walked for miles, and she saw patients who were grievously and gruesomely wounded. But I marveled most at their expressions as she leaned over them. It was a sight I will never forget."

Back home, many people criticized Eleanor's trip as a waste of time and money. It was just another political stunt. One soldier staunchly defended her by saying, "As far as our bunch is concerned we would all be willing to turn over our pay for the rest of the war to help compensate you fellows on the home front for any inconvenience you suffered by Mrs. Roosevelt's trip." Another soldier summed up her effect. "Over here," he said, "she was something."

Eleanor had lost 30 pounds during her trip. She looked and felt exhausted. The president wanted a full report from his wife on the condition of the troops. As tired as Eleanor felt, he got it, complete with some suggestions of her own. She told Franklin how the nation could best compensate the men—whose faces she had come to know—when this bitter war was done.

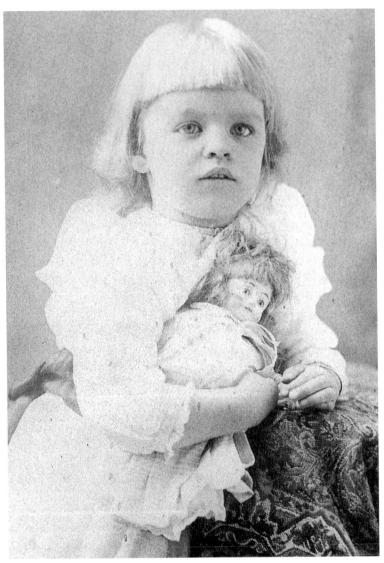

Eleanor in 1887. Her parents were New York socialites.

Chapter TWO

A TROUBLED START

ELEANOR ROOSEVELT WAS BORN IN **1884** INTO A world of wealth, glamour, and frivolity. Both her parents came from wealthy, distinguished families reaching back to colonial times. Eleanor's mother, Anna Livingston Ludlow Hall, was descended from Philip Livingston, a signer of the Declaration of Independence.

Eleanor's father, Elliott Roosevelt, was a congenial young man, but he was also deeply troubled. As a child, he and his sisters, Corinne and Anna ("Bye"), and his brother, Theodore ("Ted"), had enjoyed every advantage. But Elliott, the youngest, competed with his older brother, Ted, and it seemed Elliott could never win. After their father, Theodore Roosevelt Sr., died, Elliott began drinking.

Elliott seemed to settle down after he met "a tall slender fair-haired little beauty," as he described Anna Hall. When they married on December 1, 1883, their wedding was one of the big events of the social season in New York City. She was nineteen; he was twenty-three.

Elliott and Anna were a stunning couple. He was darkly handsome, and she was considered extravagantly beautiful. They entertained lavishly at their well-staffed house in a fashionable part of the city. Elliott went to work in one of New York's leading real estate firms and had other plans as well—to make more money, write a book, and run for political office. Somehow, though, he never seemed to make much progress on these goals.

Anna and Elliott had a lot in common, but their personalities were quite different. Elliott was tender and spontaneous. Anna belonged to what Eleanor later described as "that New York City society which thought itself all-important." Elliott's family, although well-to-do, tried to help the poor.

Eleanor was named Anna Eleanor Roosevelt when she was born on Saturday, October 11, 1884. Elliott was thrilled with the baby girl he called "a miracle from heaven." Anna, who often seemed indifferent toward her daughter, was disappointed that Eleanor was not a pretty baby. Besides, Anna had wanted a boy.

In those days, babies in wealthy families were cared for by nurses, and Anna quickly hired one. She con-

Eleanor's beautiful mother, Anna. Anna and Elliott sometimes argued about Elliott's drinking.

sidered languages important, so the nurse was French, and Eleanor's first words were French.

Eleanor's earliest memory was of being dressed up and asked to come down to meet her father's friends. They "applauded and laughed as I pirouetted before them," Eleanor recalled. "Finally, my father would pick me up and hold me high in the air." With Elliott, "I was perfectly happy," she said.

Eleanor's parents lived a fun-loving life of sailing, teas, and balls. Anna especially enjoyed dances. Eleanor loved to watch her mother dress to go out, choosing exactly the right gown among the many ordered from Paris and London. "My mother was one of the most beautiful women I have ever seen . . . ," Eleanor said. Awestruck, Eleanor was "grateful to be allowed to touch her dress or her jewels or anything that was part of the vision."

THE CENTER OF HER WORLD

Unfortunately, Elliott began drinking far too heavily. He was gentle with Eleanor, but everything else changed when he was drinking. He grew moody and depressed. He forgot promises he made to Eleanor.

One day Elliott took Eleanor for a walk. He asked her to stay outside while he stopped at his club, the Knickerbocker, for a drink. The little girl waited patiently for several hours. Finally, she saw her father carried out drunk on the arms of several men. The doorman took her home.

Sometimes Elliott was gone for weeks at a time for polo matches, hunting trips, and other sporting events. When he was away, Anna often took Eleanor to the summer home of her mother, Mary Hall, near the town of Tivoli, New York. Eleanor missed her father, but as she put it, he remained "the center of my world."

The high-ceilinged, formal house at Tivoli overlooked the Hudson River. Its fourteen bedrooms could accommodate Grandmother Hall's large family—Anna's brothers, Valentine ("Vallie") and Edward ("Eddie"), and her sisters, Edith ("Pussie"), Elizabeth ("Tissie"), and Maude. A huge library held books enough to wile away many long summer hours.

The summer of 1888 began what was perhaps one of the happiest times in Eleanor's life. Elliott was mostly sober. He and Anna were building a new house on Long Island and moved the family into a cozy cottage nearby while they oversaw its construction. Eleanor felt close to her parents there. She spent her days playing with her kitten, puppy, and chickens. Her indulgent father bragged that she got "very dirty as a general rule."

Eleanor also got to play with her Uncle Ted's daughter Alice, since Uncle Ted's summer home wasn't far away. Uncle Ted was Eleanor's godfather. He often told her she was his favorite niece. In many ways childlike himself, Uncle Ted loved to romp with all the "chicks."

In October 1888, Eleanor celebrated her fourth birthday. Elliott wrote to his sister Bye that "the funny little tot had a happy little birthday." The tot had even declared that "she loved everybody and everybody loved her."

In October 1889, Anna had a little boy and named him Elliott Jr. Like many other family members, young Elliott soon had a nickname—"Ellie."

Even with a new baby in the family, Eleanor's happy life was collapsing. Elliott had fractured his ankle that summer. Suffering severe pain, he had begun drinking again. He didn't rejoice when Ellie was born as he had for Eleanor. Instead, he spent Christmas away from them all in Bermuda. When he returned, his sisters no longer wanted him at their dinner parties because he would get drunk and embarrass them.

Elliott knew he was out of control. During the summer of 1890, he took his family to Europe, seeking help for his alcoholism. On one happy day, he took five-year-old Eleanor on a gondola ride in Venice and sang to her like the other gondoliers, which gave her, she said, "intense joy." The family traveled to Austria, where Elliott entered a sanitarium, and then to France and another sanitarium. Nothing seemed to help.

Anna, meanwhile, was expecting her third child. In 1891, she gave birth to Grace Hall (a baby boy the family called "Hall"). Then Anna told Elliott she'd had enough. She didn't want to see him for at least a year. She left Elliott in a sanitarium near Paris, took Eleanor and Eleanor's two tiny brothers, and sailed for New York.

ALWAYS AFRAID

Throughout Elliott's struggles, his sister Bye had tried to help him and Anna. Not surprisingly, Anna wanted to be near Bye in New York and so bought a house close to her. Otherwise, Anna returned to her old life. She tried to maintain the appearance of normalcy, but she suffered painful headaches. Eleanor spent hours rubbing her mother's head. But an emotional wall remained between them. Anna spent time with her three children every afternoon, but Eleanor hung back, standing in the door with her finger in her mouth. "Come in, Granny," Anna would say. Eleanor remembered Anna telling visitors, "'She's such a funny child,

so old-fashioned, we always call her 'Granny.'"
Eleanor "wanted to sink through the floor in shame."

In February 1892, Elliott returned to the United
States to enter yet another sanitarium. No one explained his condition or extended absence to Eleanor,
and she was confused. "Something was wrong with
my father," she somehow knew, yet "from my point of
view nothing could be wrong with him."

At age seven, Eleanor had not started school and
still could not read. In the fall of 1892, Anna hired a
teacher and turned an upper floor of her new house
into a school for Eleanor and a few other girls her
age. Eleanor was painfully shy and hated reciting in
front of the other girls, especially at first. When Anna
took Eleanor to parties on Saturday afternoons to
meet other children, Eleanor often broke into tears
and had to be taken home.

In fact, "anything I accomplished," she wrote later,
"had to be done across a barrier of fear." She was "always afraid of something"—afraid of the dark, of dogs
and horses and snakes. She was afraid of being
scolded.

Eleanor was also quite plain. This was a disappoint-
ment to her mother, and Eleanor knew it. "She tried
hard to bring me up well so that my manners would
compensate for my looks," Eleanor believed. Eleanor
was taught to improve her posture by walking with a
stick across her back and under her arms (in fact, she
walked ramrod straight all her life). She took dance

lessons but couldn't manage to enjoy dancing as her mother did. These efforts, Eleanor said, "only made me more keenly conscious of my shortcomings."

In late November 1892, Anna suddenly became ill with diphtheria. Eleanor was standing by a window when a cousin, Susie Parish, came to tell her some sad news. Eleanor's glamorous, twenty-nine-year-old mother had died, and Elliott was on his way home. Eight-year-old Eleanor could hardly grasp all this.

Elliott with Hall, on his lap, *Eleanor,* middle, *and Ellie,* right. *Elliott was a tender but unreliable father.*

"Death meant nothing to me," she said. "One fact wiped out everything else. My father was back."

Eleanor long remembered the encounter with her father that followed. "He sat in a big chair," she said. "He was dressed all in black, looking very sad. He held out his arms and gathered me to him." Anna had been "all the world to him," Elliott told Eleanor, "and now he had only my brothers and myself . . . he and I must keep close together."

The closeness would be in spirit only, however. Elliott agreed to allow his children to live with Grandmother Hall, as Anna had asked. Someday, Eleanor believed, she and Elliott "would have a life of our own together," but that time must wait. "When he left," she wrote, "I was all alone to keep our secret of mutual understanding and to adjust myself to my new existence."

GRANDMOTHER HALL'S

Eleanor's new home was a huge house in Manhattan, New York. Besides Eleanor and Ellie and Hall, the household consisted of Grandmother Hall, Aunt Pussie and Aunt Maude, Uncle Vallie and Uncle Eddie, and the servants.

Grandmother Hall's sons were wild and drank too much. Her daughters had not yet married. She blamed herself for their failures, believing she had been too lax a mother. She was determined to provide more discipline for her grandchildren.

The result was a somber household. Eleanor's cousin Corinne recalled that "the general attitude was 'don't do this.'" Another cousin "never wanted to go" to visit Eleanor. "There was no place to play games, unbroken gloom everywhere. We ate our suppers in silence." One of Eleanor's small pleasures was washing dishes with the butler.

And she waited for her father. He did visit and always brought presents, but she never knew when he was coming. As if she were always listening for him, she found she could hear his voice in the entryway "even in my room two long flights of stairs above." "Walking downstairs was far too slow" in her opinion. "I slid down the banisters and . . . catapulted into his arms."

In 1893 both of Eleanor's brothers got scarlet fever. Hall soon recovered. Ellie, however, "never seemed to thrive after my mother's death," Eleanor believed. Just four years old, little Ellie died. When Eleanor saw her father, she comforted him, telling him that Ellie was safe in heaven with Mother.

At Thanksgiving, Eleanor's father took her to help serve dinner at a home for homeless boys that Eleanor's grandfather, Theodore Roosevelt Sr., had helped establish. At Christmas, other family members took Eleanor to hospitals and missions in the poorest parts of the city to decorate Christmas trees and sing carols for the poor. As life moved on, Eleanor was learning the Roosevelt family values.

Elliott had been in a downward plunge for several years. On August 14, 1894, Eleanor's aunts told her the most crushing news of her difficult life. Her father was dead. Eleanor was nine.

Grandmother Hall would not allow Eleanor and two-year-old Hall to go to the funeral. So Eleanor cried herself to sleep with "no tangible thing to make death

LEAVE SOME MARK UPON THE WORLD

Eleanor wrote this essay on ambition when she was fourteen:

Is it best never to be known and to leave the world a blank as if one had never come? It must have been meant, it seems to me, that we should leave some mark upon the world and not just live [and] pass away. For what good can that do to ourselves or others? It is better to be ambitious & do something than to be unambitious and do nothing.

real," as she felt. Elliott had often disappointed Eleanor, yet he remained her dream father. If anything, the dream intensified after his death. "I knew he was dead," she wrote, "and yet I lived with him more closely, probably, than I had when he was alive."

In the following years, Grandmother Hall continued to give Eleanor and Hall a proper upbringing. Eleanor still studied with the teacher her mother had hired. She also took classes in French and in music, and she practiced dances like the waltz and the two-step. These were all necessary skills for young ladies.

Unlike other wealthy girls, however, Eleanor had few dresses, and those she had were unfashionably shapeless and short. In the 1890s, a girl's dresses were expected to get longer as she got older. Eleanor's did not. Grandmother Hall also made Eleanor wear long underwear all winter long.

Grandmother Hall was not neglecting Eleanor. If anything, Eleanor wished her grandmother would develop more interests of her own. Perhaps then she would spend less time superintending every detail of Eleanor's life.

The Halls spent much of the summer each year at their house near Tivoli. Eleanor and Hall had more freedom there. They could sneak in forbidden games, such as sliding down the roof of the ice house. They caught tadpoles in a little stream. Eleanor spent long hours reading outside. She also practiced "high-kicking" like the ballerinas she admired (even though, as Grandmother Hall told her, "no lady did anything like that").

Eleanor saw little of her father's family. She did occasionally visit Uncle Ted, his wife, Edith, and Alice and her other cousins. Uncle Ted's family was boisterous and loved outdoor games, but quiet Eleanor didn't even know how to swim. Alice, who could be wicked, found Eleanor too well behaved. But Uncle Ted still adored her.

When Eleanor was fourteen, she went to her first party with boys her own age. She found the experience painful. She was gangly and awkward and still unsure of her dancing. Worse, her grandmother dressed her in a short white dress with blue bows on the shoulders. It made Eleanor look like a child. Meanwhile, Alice swept around in a sophisticated ankle-length gown. Thankfully, Eleanor's fifth cousin found her and asked her to dance. At that moment, she registered eternal gratitude for the kindness of Franklin Delano Roosevelt.

In 1899 Eleanor, above, *encountered a gifted teacher, Marie Souvestre.*

Chapter **THREE**

NEW LIFE AT ALLENSWOOD

IN THE AUTUMN OF **1899,** WHEN ELEANOR WAS almost fifteen, Grandmother Hall decided she was ready for finishing school. Finishing schools taught the polished manners and other social skills that prepared wealthy young women to take their places as wives in high society. Well-to-do women of that era rarely had careers. With Aunt Tissie as chaperone, Eleanor sailed to England to enter Allenswood, a finishing school near London. Her bags were packed with hand-me-down dresses from her aunts, made over to fit her. At least Grandmother Hall gave Eleanor an allowance to cover small extra expenses.

Eleanor soon discovered that Allenswood's thirty-five to forty students followed a busy daily schedule. Before classes each morning, they prepared everything in their rooms for inspection, from closets to bureau drawers. They ate breakfast and then, no matter what the weather, they took a brisk walk. German, Latin, literature, history, study time, and more exercise followed. Sometimes the day ended with dancing. The girls were required to speak French all day long, even though most of them were English speaking.

Eleanor felt lost at first. Allenswood had many rules that had to be strictly followed, but Eleanor quickly adapted. "If I lived up to the rules and told the truth," she found, "there was nothing to fear." And French was no problem—Eleanor had begun learning it as a toddler and spoke it fluently.

In addition, Eleanor discovered a new friend, the headmistress of Allenswood, Mademoiselle Marie Souvestre. A distinguished woman of sixty-five, Mlle. Souvestre sometimes invited a few girls—including Eleanor—into her study, where she read poems, plays, and stories to them. Eleanor called these times "red-letter days."

Mlle. Souvestre gave Eleanor another special honor by asking her to sit opposite her at the table. Eleanor listened to the free-flowing conversations between Mlle. Souvestre and her friends at dinner and found herself repeating their ideas later. "I had no real knowledge of the thing I was talking about," she realized. But she could use her quick wit to "use their knowledge as my own."

Eleanor, in back row, third from right, *and classmates at Allenswood in 1900. Eleanor made many friends at Allenswood.*

Eleanor and a school friend spent the Christmas of 1899 with friends in Paris. Mlle. Souvestre was also vacationing in Paris and spent a few days with the girls. She encouraged Eleanor, who was still wearing hand-me-downs, to get at least one new dress. Eleanor gladly followed the advice. "If Mlle. Souvestre thought I should buy a dress I could have it," she concluded. Soon she possessed a fashionable, dark red dress made just for her by a Parisian dressmaker. "I probably got more satisfaction out of it," she wrote many years later, "than from any dress I have had since."

Eleanor returned to the United States for the summer of 1900. She was relieved to return to Allenswood that fall. All that school year and the next, she continued to thrive there. She even got to travel with Mlle.

Souvestre, who often took older students abroad with her when she traveled.

On one trip to Italy, Mlle. Souvestre put Eleanor in charge of all the practical details—checking train schedules, buying tickets, and even packing the luggage. In Florence, Mlle. Souvestre gave Eleanor a guidebook and sent her to explore the city on foot. According to Mlle. Souvestre, "the only way to know a city is to walk its streets," Eleanor explained. Again Eleanor felt a burst of confidence.

According to Eleanor, getting to know Mlle. Souvestre was "one of the most momentous things" in her education. At Allenswood, she said, "I felt that I was starting a new life, free from all my former sins." Eleanor was not expected to make up for her lack of beauty with perfect, proper, predictable behavior. "Never again," wrote Eleanor, "would I be the rigid little person I had been theretofore."

Eleanor spent three years in all at Allenswood. She was seventeen when she returned home in the summer of 1902. It was time, her grandmother had decided, for Eleanor's "coming out" as a New York debutante.

THE DEBUTANTE

Eleanor was now the niece of the president of the United States. Uncle Ted had been elected vice president, but he became president in September 1901, when President William McKinley had been assassinated.

But Eleanor found many other things at home had not changed. Again when she went out, an aunt, her maid, or another chaperone always accompanied her. Her uncles still drank too much. If anything, they had become more frightening. Eleanor often locked herself in her bedroom in order to feel safe.

Aunt Tissie sent Eleanor a wardrobe of stylish new clothes from Paris. But even so, it was difficult to make her into an elegant debutante. She was tall, didn't dance well, and didn't know many people.

That summer, as Eleanor waited for the round of gala events she was expected to attend as a debutante, Franklin Roosevelt spotted her on a train to Tivoli. He invited her to join him and his mother, Sara Delano Roosevelt. Sara and Franklin were traveling to Sara's country estate near Hyde Park, a small town in up-state New York. Franklin's parents had been fond of Eleanor's parents, especially her father, who had been Franklin's godfather.

Sara was waiting for Franklin in the train's parlor car. Franklin's father, James Roosevelt, had died two years earlier. Yet Sara was still dressed in black mourning clothes, including a heavy veil that fell from her hat to the floor.

The two distant cousins saw each other again that autumn. Franklin was attending Harvard University in nearby Cambridge, Massachusetts, and sometimes met Eleanor for lunch or tea when he was in New York. Eleanor enjoyed Franklin's lively conversation.

A ball at the famous Waldorf Astoria Hotel in December was Eleanor's first significant debutante event.
In striking contrast to Eleanor's pleasant encounters
with Franklin, she felt "utter agony" amidst the swirl
of beautiful girls and their escorts at the ball. In her
words, she was "not a belle," and the ball made her
realize this all too well. Had she known beforehand
how she would react, she said, "I would never have
had the courage to go." She went home early.

To celebrate New Year's Eve at the end of 1902,
President Teddy Roosevelt hosted a party at the White
House in Washington, D.C. Eleanor stayed there with
her cousin Alice. Franklin Roosevelt had also been invited to the party; he stayed with Eleanor's Aunt Bye.
On New Years' Day, Eleanor, Franklin, and other
guests attended a reception at the White House, had
dinner, and then went to the theater. Franklin noted
in his diary that he sat near Eleanor.

Franklin's half brother Rosy Roosevelt invited
Eleanor to Franklin's birthday party in February 1903.
Twice that summer, Eleanor traveled to Hyde Park to
join Franklin and some of his friends. In August
Franklin and his mother invited Eleanor and other
friends to their home on Campobello, a Canadian island off the coast of Maine. The young people sailed,
went on hayrides, and took long walks.

Throughout 1903, Eleanor attended rounds of dinners, parties, and dances. Aunt Tissie and her husband, Stanley Mortimer, gave a party for Eleanor that

included dancing at a fashionable restaurant. Aunt Pussie hosted several luncheons and dinners for her. Eleanor was making friends and beginning to enjoy these social occasions.

Boys in well-to-do families usually left home for boarding school when they were twelve. In the fall of 1903, Hall was old enough to leave for Groton, the same private boy's boarding school that Franklin had attended. Grandmother Hall had become quite reclusive, staying in her own rooms for days at a time, and responsibility for Hall had slipped more and more into Eleanor's hands. Like a good parent, Eleanor got Hall settled and visited him regularly for the next six years while he attended Groton.

That same fall, Eleanor joined the Consumers League, an organization lobbying for labor laws to

Eleanor in her debutante portrait, 1902. She had blue eyes, golden hair, and a willowy figure.

help poor working people. The league was just one of many reform efforts under way in the United States at the turn of the last century. At that time, many women and children earned meager wages by laboring as many as ninety-six hours a week. The Consumers League wanted a limit of sixty hours.

Eleanor was asked to check on the working conditions of children who made artificial feathers and flowers. Since many of the children did this work at home, Eleanor would have to visit them there in order to investigate. At first, she hesitated. "I felt I had no right to invade their private dwellings," she wrote. "I was frightened to death." Nonetheless, she walked up the stairs of her first tenement. There she found tiny children, some just four and five years old, bent over their work. In order to earn what their families needed, these little ones labored away "until they dropped with fatigue," Eleanor discovered.

Debutantes were also automatically members of the Junior League, an organization of wealthy young women who did charitable work. Eleanor was assigned to teach calisthenics and dancing at a settlement house. Located in a poor part of town on Rivington Street, the settlement house served as a community center for residents of the neighborhood.

Franklin had already received his diploma from Harvard that June, but he had returned for a fourth year that fall to serve as editor of the *Crimson*, the school paper. He and Eleanor had been writing to each other often. They attended many of the same parties, and sometimes when he was in New York, he dropped by the settlement house to take Eleanor home. "Gosh," he told her once when he was in the neighborhood, "I didn't know anyone lived like that."

Eleanor thought of Franklin as a friend. She didn't believe he was courting her, and she considered herself too plain to interest anyone. But she had soft blue eyes and an intelligent manner. Like Eleanor, other people also missed the fact that Franklin was falling in love, even though he clearly enjoyed Eleanor's company.

In October Franklin proposed. Eleanor was only nineteen. He was just twenty-one. Even so, she "never even thought that we were both young and inexperienced." Most of Eleanor's friends were already married or planning their weddings. Eleanor too "felt the urge to be a part of the stream of life," as she put it. Franklin's proposal, surprising as it might have been, "seemed entirely natural," she said. She accepted.

Eleanor promptly told her grandmother the news. When Grandmother Hall asked if Eleanor was sure she really was in love, Eleanor solemnly answered, "Yes." To Franklin, she wrote, "Everything is changed for me now. I am so happy. Oh! So happy & I love you dearly."

Franklin felt the same. When he told his mother about the engagement the following month, he assured her, "I am the happiest man just now in the world. Likewise the luckiest."

Franklin, Sara, and Eleanor on the grounds of Campobello in May 1905

Sara, however, was not eager to give up her only son and asked the couple to keep the engagement secret for one year. Then, if they still felt the same about each other, they could announce it. Eleanor and Franklin were not happy about Sara's plan, but they agreed to it.

Both Eleanor and Sara wanted their relationship to be a warm one. As Eleanor and Franklin waited, Eleanor and Sara began spending time together. They met for lunch or went shopping, trying to get to know each other better.

At the end of November 1904, Eleanor and Franklin finally announced their plans. Everyone was thrilled—with the possible exception of Sara. Grandmother Hall wrote Franklin to say she would miss Eleanor, but she was thankful that Eleanor was going to marry "such a fine man as I believe you to be." Eleanor's Uncle Ted wrote Franklin, "I am as fond of Eleanor as if she were my daughter; and I like you, and trust you, and believe in you." Even Sara accepted Eleanor and supported Franklin's decision.

Uncle Ted was elected president that same November. In March 1905, the engaged couple traveled to Washington, D.C., to attend his inauguration. Eleanor assumed she was witnessing the last inauguration of a member of her family. Despite the grandness of the event, she confessed that "Uncle Ted's campaign and reelection had meant little to me except in general interest." Her life was "totally unpolitical."

Franklin, on the other hand, was keenly interested in politics. He had been brought up in a strongly Democratic family, but he had voted—the very first vote he'd ever cast in a presidential election—for a Republican. According to Franklin, Teddy Roosevelt was "a better Democrat than the Democratic candidates."

Eleanor posed alone for this wedding portrait.

Chapter **FOUR**

A PROPER POLITICAL WIFE

UNCLE TED AND AUNT EDITH OFFERED TO LET
Eleanor have her wedding at the White House.
Eleanor chose instead to get married at the home of
her cousin, Susie Parish, in New York City. She did
ask Uncle Ted to give her away. He would be in New
York for the city's annual St. Patrick's Day parade on
March 17, and the wedding date was set to coincide.
Eleanor's mother's birthday was also on March 17.

That day, Eleanor was "decked out beyond descrip-
tion," as she put it. Her six bridesmaids wore hair or-
naments that resembled the Roosevelt crest. The
ushers wore diamond tie pins in the same design.
Franklin had designed a gold watch for Eleanor with
her initials set in diamonds. At her throat was a diamond

crescent that had belonged to her mother and a collar with diamond bars, given to her by Sara.

After the service, Uncle Ted kissed the bride and joked to the groom, "Well, Franklin, there's nothing like keeping the name in the family." When Uncle Ted walked into the dining room for refreshments, almost everyone forgot Eleanor and Franklin and followed him. Franklin took Eleanor's arm and smiled, "Well, we might as well join the party."

Franklin and Eleanor couldn't leave for a honeymoon right away since Franklin was enrolled in law school at Columbia University in Manhattan. Several months later, however, they traveled to Europe. In Venice, Eleanor rode in a gondola again, this time with Franklin. The young couple also strolled along the river in Paris, toured the Swiss Alps, and visited friends in England. Eleanor felt secure at Franklin's side. In fact, Eleanor felt she was becoming "an entirely dependent person," a change that was, as she said, "a pleasant contrast to my former life."

Something else had also changed. By the time Eleanor and Franklin left Europe to sail home, she was pregnant.

MOTHERHOOD

Back in New York, Eleanor's mother-in-law had acquired and furnished a house for her son and his wife to live in after the honeymoon. Sara had even hired a cook, housemaid, and butler for them. It seemed

Eleanor had little say in establishing her first home, but if that bothered her, she didn't admit it.

Franklin continued law school, and Eleanor returned to her work at the settlement house on Rivington Street and with the Consumers League. Eleanor spent much of her leisure time with Sara and usually had at least one meal with her each day.

On May 3, 1906, Eleanor gave birth to a daughter, Anna Eleanor, named after Eleanor's mother and Eleanor herself. Eleanor, who had never had any interest in dolls or in caring for younger children, had no idea what to do with a newborn. "I knew absolutely nothing about handling or feeding a baby," she claimed. She hired a series of nurses to help her.

She wanted to continue her volunteer work but quit when Sara advised against it because Eleanor risked "bringing the diseases of the slums" home with her. Sara certainly supported Franklin when he took a job with a law firm. It was even fine for him to go off on sprees with his Harvard friends. Eleanor, however, must act like a proper wife and mother.

On December 23, 1907, when little Anna was about eighteen months old, Eleanor and Franklin had a second child. They named him James, after Franklin's father. Sara decided the new parents needed a bigger house, so she bought a plot of land on East 65th Street. She had two houses built there—one for Franklin and Eleanor and one for herself. The doors in the dining rooms and drawing rooms of each house

could be opened to join each other. The doors between the two houses were seldom locked, and Sara
could come and go as she wished. Sometimes Sara
seemed to be in charge of both households. She chose
the nurses, toys, and clothes for Eleanor's children.

Shortly after moving into the new house, Franklin
found his young wife weeping in front of her dressing
table. He asked her what was wrong. She did not like
living "in a house that was not in any way mine," she
told him, "one that I had done nothing about and
which did not represent the way I wanted to live."
Franklin didn't understand and gently said she was
"quite mad." She would feel better in a little while.

Instead, Eleanor grew more withdrawn over time.
Rather than express her feelings, she developed what
she called the "maddening habit" of "simply shutting
up like a clam." This left her appearing "too obvi-
ously humble and meek," as she put it, as well as
"feeling like a martyr and acting like one."

Eleanor continued to shy away from social situa-
tions. When she attended parties with Franklin, she
usually left before he was ready to go. She encouraged
him to stay and enjoy the festivities—which her
charming, outgoing husband usually did.

Eleanor and Franklin often took their youngsters to
Sara's summer retreat at Campobello. Franklin's family and friends relaxed by playing tennis, golf, and
other sports, but Eleanor rarely joined the fun.
Franklin urged Eleanor to learn tennis, but she wasn't

Franklin and Eleanor relax at Campobello, 1910.

any good at it. She self-consciously believed that she annoyed other people when she tried to play, so she quit trying. She also tried to learn golf, since Franklin loved the game. She remembered, "After watching me for a few minutes, [Franklin] remarked that he thought I might as well give it up!" She did. Eleanor did learn how to sail, however, even though she had a fear of water.

On March 18, 1909, Eleanor gave birth to another little boy, Franklin Jr. Although he was a large baby—11 pounds at birth—he was a fragile child, and he died the following November. The family buried him at Hyde Park.

For a while, Eleanor blamed herself for the baby's death, vaguely feeling she had lost him because she hadn't cared for him enough. Eleanor had other children—Anna was age three-and-a-half, and James was almost two. Yet Eleanor felt no strong maternal instinct. A friend of hers, Joseph Lash, later wrote, "The baby's death reinforced her sense of inadequacy as a woman and as a mother."

By the spring of 1910, Eleanor was pregnant again. She and Sara and the children spent much of that summer at Hyde Park and Campobello. Eleanor returned to New York ahead of the group to prepare for the birth. Little Elliott, named after Eleanor's father, was born on September 23, 1910.

ENTERING POLITICAL LIFE

At this point, Franklin was working for Carter, Ledyard and Milburn, a well-respected New York law firm. He yearned for a life of public service, however. He began meeting regularly with leaders of the Democratic Party. Two weeks after Elliott's birth, party leaders nominated Franklin for the state senate.

Franklin campaigned exhaustively, stopping at every village and farm. On election day, he won by 1,500 votes—a significant victory for a Democrat in a solidly Republican district.

As a state senator, Franklin would need to live in Albany, the capital of New York. He and Eleanor bought a large brownstone house and moved the family there.

For the first time, Eleanor had chosen her own home, one where she would not be under Sara's watchful eye. Over the next two years, Eleanor met hundreds of new people.

Her home became a gathering spot for liberal Democrats. Eleanor discovered that she enjoyed being married to a man near the center of public activity. Slender and tall (five foot eleven), she looked attractive in the styles of the time. Her warm personality more than made up for any physical imperfections.

Eleanor's brother Hall married Margaret Richardson of Boston in June 1912. Eleanor had mixed feelings about the marriage: it seemed as though her son, not her brother, was being married.

Later that summer, both Eleanor and Franklin contracted typhoid fever, and both were too sick to campaign for Franklin's reelection. Franklin won anyway, thanks, in part, to a new political adviser, Louis Howe. Eleanor didn't like Howe very much, and Sara described him as an "ugly, dirty little man." Howe was intensely loyal to Franklin, however, and he had a brilliant political mind.

Woodrow Wilson was elected president that same fall. After Wilson's inauguration in March 1913, Franklin, who had campaigned for Wilson, was offered a job once held by Eleanor's Uncle Ted, assistant secretary of the navy. Franklin was on his way to Washington, D.C.—and to a position of national prominence.

WASHINGTON WAYS

In the autumn of 1913, the family moved into a comfortable red brick house on a tree-shaded street in Washington. Eleanor liked to eat breakfast in its small back garden.

From Aunt Bye, who lived nearby, Eleanor learned the rituals of proper political wives in Washington. Wives must stop at one another's homes regularly, Eleanor discovered. They wore white gloves and carried calling cards to leave behind them if they found no one home. Eleanor made calls every day but Wednesdays, when she stayed home to receive (although she was sure, at first, that no one would come to see her).

Franklin and Eleanor were popular guests at dinners and parties. They attended many receptions at the White House. Life became so hectic that Eleanor hired a social secretary, Lucy Mercer. Only Sunday evenings were quiet. Eleanor and "Pa," as the children called Franklin, stayed home and dined with a few close friends. Eleanor made scrambled eggs in a chafing dish at the table.

Eleanor and Franklin had another little boy on August 17, 1914. They named him Franklin Jr., just as they had named the baby who had died. On March 13, 1916, their last child, John Aspinwall, was born.

The Roosevelt children had the best governesses and attended the best schools Eleanor could find. She read to her children every day and heard their prayers every night. In the summer, she took them fishing and sailing at Hyde Park or Campobello. She was pleased when they learned to swim, because she had been afraid to swim. She wanted them to conquer their fears.

Eleanor with her children Elliott, left, *John,* second from left, *Franklin Jr.,* middle, *and Anna,* right, *at Campobello in 1920. Their dog's name was Chief.*

Warm mothering did not come naturally to Eleanor, however. She had become a strict disciplinarian who was distressed by her children's "wildness." Sara seemed to be in constant competition with Eleanor and indulged the children. "The best way to circumvent Pa and Mummy. . . ," James later wrote, "was to appeal to Granny."

Franklin was no help. "Let the chicks run wild at Hyde Park," he told Eleanor, sounding just like her famous uncle. "It won't hurt them." Besides, the assistant secretary of the navy had other things on his mind. The nations of Europe had become embroiled in a great war, and Franklin was focused on preparing the United States to defend itself if necessary.

WAR AND OTHER SORROWS

On April 2, 1917, President Woodrow Wilson asked Congress for a declaration of war allowing the United States to join the war in Europe. Wilson had tried to keep the nation neutral. But German submarines had sunk ships carrying Americans, and a German plot against the United States had been uncovered. Pushed too far, Wilson declared, "The world must be made safe for democracy."

When the United States entered World War I, Franklin and Eleanor took on many new responsibilities. Franklin had to oversee the mobilization of the navy. Eleanor volunteered at the Red Cross canteen. Soldiers passing through Washington on their way overseas could stop at the canteen for coffee, soup, and sandwiches. Eleanor often worked—from early morning until after midnight.

In July 1917, Franklin sailed for Europe to visit the front lines. He returned in September, ill with double pneumonia. While unpacking his luggage, Eleanor found a packet of letters and immediately recognized the handwriting of Lucy Mercer, her own social secretary. Lucy had written love letters to Franklin.

Eleanor immediately offered Franklin a divorce. A divorce would have created a scandal, however, and ruined Franklin's career. Besides, Franklin was used to a lifestyle that depended on money he received from Sara, and she threatened to cut him off without a penny if he left Eleanor and the children. Franklin declined Eleanor's offer and promised never to see Lucy again.

Eleanor's self-confidence had plummeted. She lost weight, rarely smiled, and avoided looking directly at the camera when photographs were taken. She tried to forgive Franklin, but the marriage—and Eleanor—had changed forever. As Eleanor put it, "The bottom dropped out of my own particular world, and I faced myself, my surroundings, my world, honestly for the first time."

Eleanor and Franklin in 1920. The two struggled to rebuild their marriage after Franklin had an affair.

Chapter **FIVE**

HITTING HER STRIDE

WORLD WAR I ENDED ON NOVEMBER 11, 1918.
Although the United States had joined the fight long
after it began, the costs of war had come to thirty-two
billion dollars. More than 130,000 American soldiers
had died. Thousands more had been wounded and
still lay in military hospital beds.

Eleanor's focus shifted to conditions at the military
hospitals near her. At St. Elizabeth's, a hospital for the
mentally ill, she found shell-shocked veterans locked
in what she called "cagelike porches," with no chance
for exercise or recreation. Thanks to her efforts, Congress approved additional funds for the hospital.

Early in 1919, Franklin began the task of closing
down American army bases in Europe and asked

Eleanor to accompany him there. Shortly after they sailed, they learned that Theodore Roosevelt had died. Eleanor felt the loss keenly. "A great personality had gone from . . . the life of his people," she wrote.

In France, Eleanor was horrified by the towns left ruined by the war. Nothing remained of Boulogne Wood but a "few bare sticks," she wrote to a friend. "What the men who fought there lived through is inconceivable." President Wilson was urging the United States to join a new international organization, the League of Nations, to help prevent future wars. Eleanor's encounter with the destruction of World War I gave her an earnest—and lasting—hope that he would succeed.

As Franklin and Eleanor traveled, they tried to rebuild their relationship. Eleanor struggled to voice her feelings to Franklin, but it wasn't easy. "I do not think I have ever felt so strangely as in the past year . . . ," she wrote in her diary. "All my self-confidence is gone."

Once Eleanor was home again, however, she began to take charge. "The life you live is your own," she wrote. When she noticed that many black workers were being fired to create jobs for returning white veterans, she replaced her own white servants with a black staff. Sara and New York society did not approve.

Eleanor and Franklin spent part of the summer of 1919 at Hyde Park, where things did not go well. Eleanor and Sara argued frequently. When the visit ended, Eleanor told Franklin, "I feel as though someone has taken a ton of bricks off me."

In August 1919, Grandmother Hall died. Eleanor, at age thirty-four, realized by now what a sacrifice her grandmother had made for her and her brothers. Still, Eleanor didn't want to follow Grandmother Hall's example. "Even when I was young," she wrote, "I determined that I would never be dependent on my children by allowing all my interests to center in them." Instead, Eleanor believed, "Life is meant to be lived."

Eleanor grew increasingly independent in decisions about her children. When her oldest child, Anna, began getting poor grades, she decided Anna's school was too "stuffy." James was not doing well either, so she began getting up early in the morning to have him say his lessons to her before school.

Eleanor spent her thirty-fifth birthday alone. For Franklin's birthday, she held a party and asked guests to come dressed as a character in a book. The two still attended many obligatory dinner parties. Eleanor tried to enjoy them—Franklin certainly did—but found she couldn't.

In 1920 Eleanor was staying with the children at Campobello for the summer while Franklin attended the Democratic National Convention in San Francisco. James M. Cox won the presidential nomination and asked Franklin to be his running mate. Franklin accepted, even though the Democrats did not have much chance of winning. He wanted the national attention he would receive by running for the vice presidency.

The main issue of the campaign was U.S. membership in the League of Nations. James Cox and
Franklin urged the United States to join. The Republican candidate, Warren G. Harding, and his running
mate, Calvin Coolidge, didn't. Harding urged a "return
to normalcy," which meant staying out of the problems of other nations. Americans were tired of international entanglements after the staggering losses of
World War I, so Harding seemed likely to win.

On August 26, the Nineteenth Amendment to the
U.S. Constitution was passed. Women had won, for
the first time, the right to vote in a national election.
Not surprisingly, candidates' wives suddenly took on a
new importance in political campaigns. Franklin
asked Eleanor to join him on a campaign trip across
the country.

At each stop during the four-week train trip,
Franklin made the same speech on the issues. Eleanor
dutifully listened with what she called "apparently
rapt attention," although she heard it over and over.
With each repetition, the speeches got longer.
Franklin's aides began standing behind the crowd,
waving at him to stop. When that failed, Eleanor
yanked his coattails.

Franklin's staff relaxed together every night, dis-
cussing the campaign and playing cards. As the only
woman, Eleanor often felt isolated and useless. Louis
Howe sensed this and began knocking on the door of
her stateroom at the end of the day, "asking if he

might discuss a speech with me," Eleanor remembered. He convinced Eleanor that her opinions mattered and that she contributed immensely to her husband's campaign.

As expected, James Cox and Franklin lost the election, but at least the national exposure had been good for Franklin's career. The Roosevelts returned to New York City, where Franklin formed a new law firm and hired a secretary, Marguerite ("Missy") LeHand.

Eleanor dreaded returning to a life of "nothing but teas and luncheons and dinners to take up my time." She had five children aged three to fourteen, but her life was somewhat detached from theirs. When the children weren't in school, they spent much of their time with nurses and governesses.

To stay busy, Eleanor turned to a new organization, the League of Women Voters. She accepted responsibility for reports on national legislation, even though at first she doubted her ability to do the work.

She quickly made new friends in the organization. Eleanor liked Elizabeth Read, a lawyer, at once. "She gave me a sense of confidence," Eleanor said. Elizabeth shared a house with Esther Lape, a professor and writer, in Greenwich Village in New York. Elizabeth and Esther led very different lives from the society matrons Eleanor knew, and Eleanor welcomed the change.

Eleanor still clashed often with Sara, but the clashes bothered her less. After one argument, Eleanor wrote,

"I should be ashamed of myself and I'm not." Sara discouraged Eleanor's friendship with Elizabeth and Esther, but Eleanor was "drifting far afield from the old influences . . . ," as she put it, and "thinking things out for myself." As Eleanor's fondness for Elizabeth and Esther grew, she began spending one night a week with them in Greenwich Village.

A Turn for the Worse

During the summer of 1921, Eleanor, children, and friends relaxed at Campobello. Franklin joined them in August. He played tennis and baseball with the children, took them sailing, and worked on model boats with Louis Howe. On August 10, after a brisk swim, he complained of aches and chills and went to bed early.

The next day, he couldn't move his left leg. By that afternoon, he couldn't move his right leg. His temperature was high. Eleanor sent for a doctor, who thought Franklin had caught a cold. By Friday, however, Franklin was paralyzed from the chest down. A specialist finally arrived and identified the illness as infantile paralysis—polio.

The diagnosis was a frightening one. Polio is a serious disease that can result in permanent paralysis. No one knew to what extent Franklin would recover.

For the next three weeks, Eleanor slept on a couch in Franklin's room, bathed him, massaged him, and cared for his every need until a nurse could be found to care for him. The hurt she had felt was replaced with tender concern.

When Franklin was well enough, he was moved to Presbyterian Hospital in New York. He couldn't walk, but he thought that before long he would be moving around on crutches and working again. Sara believed Franklin would never be able to resume his career and wanted him to retire and live at Hyde Park as a country gentleman.

Eleanor and Louis Howe disagreed with Sara. They encouraged Franklin to work hard on his recovery so that he could return to his old life. If Sara had her way, Eleanor would remain under her mother-in-law's domination for the rest of her life. By resisting Sara, Eleanor was beginning to stand on her own two feet.

Franklin did not retire to Hyde Park. He returned to the Roosevelt's house in New York. A nurse moved in to take care of him. Louis Howe moved in as well to help Franklin with his business and political affairs.

After these guests, the children, the servants, and the children's nurses were given bedrooms, no room remained for Eleanor. She slept on a bed in one of the boys' rooms and dressed in Franklin's bathroom. With a house full of people and an invalid husband, she said, "I was too busy to need a room."

Eleanor was adept at putting up a strong front, but the stress of Franklin's illness took a toll. One day as she was reading to Franklin Jr. and John, she suddenly found herself sobbing. "I could not think why...," she said, "nor could I stop." Louis tried to comfort her, but "he gave it up as a bad job." Eleanor cried well into the evening.

Not until the following summer did Franklin learn to walk again and then only with the help of crutches. He walked a little every day to build his confidence. "Each new thing he did," Eleanor realized, "took not only determination but great physical effort."

LIFE AFTER POLIO

Franklin eventually returned to his law practice, but his family had to accept that he would never fully recover the use of his legs. He sometimes steadied himself on the arm of his son James when he needed to get out of a car or climb up to a platform. Otherwise, he used a wheelchair to get around.

Eleanor considered the effect of Franklin's illness on her youngest sons. "I had two young boys who had to

Franklin and Eleanor at Hyde Park in 1922. After Franklin was struck with polio, Eleanor insisted that he continue to work.

learn to do the things that boys must do—swim and ride and camp . . . ," she said. "If [they] were going to have a normal existence without a father to do these things with them, I would have to become a good deal more companionable." She took the boys camping and, at age thirty-seven, finally learned to swim.

Louis Howe encouraged Eleanor to keep the Roosevelt name prominent during Franklin's recuperation. At first she didn't see how she could, but she wanted to be useful. She decided to join the Women's Trade Union League, which was fighting for better working conditions for women. She also accepted an invitation to speak to the women's division of the Democratic State Committee, even though she had never before made a speech to any sizable gathering.

She was not a good speaker. Since she was nervous, her voice sounded high and shrill. She laughed even when there was nothing to laugh at. As she gave more and more speeches, Louis Howe coached her, advising, "Have something you want to say, say it, and sit down." Eventually she improved.

Both Eleanor and Franklin attended the Democratic National Convention in the summer of 1924. She wanted to see where the Democratic Party's newest voting members—women—would stand. "They stood outside the door of all important meetings and waited," she discovered. Eleanor was able to submit some resolutions, "but how much consideration they got was veiled in mystery."

All that year, Franklin traveled frequently, seeking a cure for his crippled legs. In the autumn of 1924, in Warm Springs, Georgia, he discovered a rundown resort with a swimming pool with water from the area's warm, natural springs. Franklin found he could swim for long periods in the soothing water without becoming tired or chilled. Buoyed in both body and spirit, Franklin bought the resort and turned it into a rehabilitation center for polio victims.

President Harding had died in 1923, and his vice president, Calvin Coolidge, had become president. To no one's surprise, Coolidge won the presidency in the fall election of 1924.

In 1925 Eleanor supported a bill limiting the workweek for women to forty-eight hours. She testified before the New York state legislature, but the members later refused to even vote on the bill. When Republican women protested the legislature's lack of action, Eleanor considered their stand "a vindication of the value of women in politics."

Little by little, Eleanor became acquainted with many progressive, politically active women. In 1927 Eleanor and two women friends from the women's division of the Democratic Party—Nancy Cook and Marian Dickerman—purchased Todhunter School, a private school for girls. Dickerman became the school's principal, and Eleanor taught history, literature, and current events. To make government seem "real and alive" to her students, she took them to

Eleanor, Marian Dickerman, middle, *and Nancy Cook,* right, *in 1926. Franklin later built a cottage at Hyde Park for Eleanor and these friends.*

courtrooms, slums, markets, and other places that would broaden their experience.

Eleanor was hitting her stride. In May 1927, she wrote an article called "What I Want Most Out of Life" for *Success* magazine. Women should "guard against the emptiness and loneliness that enter some women's lives after their children are grown," she wrote. Her own daughter, Anna, had just turned twenty-one. James was nineteen. Encouraging women to enter politics, she pointed out "the opportunity for doing something useful." And after all, what Eleanor wanted most out of life, she said, was to be useful. "In no other way," wrote the emerging feminist, "can true happiness be obtained."

To steady himself, Franklin takes the arm of his son John in Albany, New York.

Chapter **SIX**

RELUCTANT
FIRST LADY

ELEANOR AND FRANKLIN'S CHILDREN WERE GROW-
ing up. As was customary for boys of well-to-do parents, their sons left for boarding school when they
were twelve. In September 1928, Eleanor took her
youngest, twelve-year-old John, to Groton. "When it
came to the last child," she said, saying good-bye "was
particularly hard."

That fall, Franklin ran for governor of New York. On
election day in November, the Republicans won the
presidency yet again when Herbert Hoover defeated Al
Smith. Even without Democratic "coattails" to carry
Franklin to victory, however, he won his race.

Once again the Roosevelts moved to Albany, this
time to the governor's mansion. Eleanor chose "the

grandest sunny room" for Franklin and ordered a swimming pool built for him. For herself she chose only a former sitting room and study. She would be spending part of each week in New York anyway.

Eleanor loved teaching at the Todhunter School and had decided to continue. She began taking the train to New York every Sunday, teaching her classes for three days, and then returning to Albany on Wednesday afternoons.

Eleanor also helped Franklin in many ways. She played hostess at teas, gave lectures, and answered volumes of mail. He couldn't inspect the interiors of state institutions because walking was so difficult for him, so she served as his legs.

At first she reported far too little information. "I would tell him what was on the menu for the day," she explained, "and he would ask: 'Did you look to see whether the inmates were actually getting that food?'"

Eleanor learned to watch for telling details. If she found folding beds stashed in closets during the day, she could guess that the beds filled the corridors at night—a situation that did not meet the standards for the care of patients. Eventually Eleanor became what she called a "fairly expert reporter on state institutions."

Eleanor often traveled alone to do inspections, lectures, and radio programs. She refused to use a chauffeur or a limousine. Instead, she drove herself in her own car. Franklin, concerned about her safety, finally insisted she at least have a bodyguard.

Eleanor and her bodyguard, Earl Miller, in Warm Springs, Georgia. The two became good friends.

Franklin assigned state trooper Earl Miller. Earl, who had once been a prize-winning swimmer and boxer, was an unlikely companion for Eleanor. Before long, however, the two became close friends. Earl coached Eleanor in tennis, revived her interest in horseback riding, and taught her how to shoot a pistol. Earl called Eleanor "the Lady" and seemed "unfailingly attentive and chivalrous," according to her. When the two of them appeared to inspect a hospital, prison, or other project—with Miller in full dress uniform—"they made a formidable team."

TUMULTUOUS CHANGES

On October 29, 1929, the New York Stock Exchange crashed, ushering in the beginning of the Great Depression. Factories closed, businesses collapsed, and many people lost their jobs.

Eleanor believed something must be fundamentally wrong with the American system since it had led to such cruel conditions. She told the New York City League of Women Voters that emergency measures were not enough. More creative, long-term solutions were needed. "We must be prepared to meet things with open minds," she told her audience. She repeated the idea of keeping "an open and speculative mind" in an article in *Vogue* magazine.

In November 1930, Franklin won reelection by the largest vote ever cast for a Democratic governor in New York. His easy victory and continued popularity over the next two years made him a prime candidate for the presidential nomination in 1932.

The Roosevelts were at the governor's mansion with friends in the summer of 1932 when a message arrived from the Democratic National Convention in Chicago. Franklin had been nominated for president. As people cheered and hugged each other and reporters tumbled into the house, Eleanor announced, "I'm going to make some bacon and eggs."

Eleanor was carrying a secret she confessed only years later. "I did not want my husband to be president," she admitted. If Franklin won the presidency, Eleanor believed she would surely face "the end of any personal life of my own." As First Lady, she would have to stop teaching. She didn't want to do that. By earning her own money, she could "do things in which I was personally interested."

Eleanor and Franklin quickly flew to Chicago. Franklin spoke to the convention, becoming the first nominee for the presidency to address a national convention. In his speech, he promised a "New Deal" for the American people. Franklin's huge smile and stirring ideas brought cheers.

DUMPING THE REPUBLICANS

As campaigning began, President Herbert Hoover seemed, if anything, to be deepening the nation's problems. Shortly after the convention, twenty-five thousand veterans of World War I came to Washington. They asked the government to pay them bonuses promised to them in 1924. The bonuses weren't due until 1945, but many of the men were jobless and hungry. They needed the money. The "bonus marchers," as they were called, pitched a camp of tents and shacks made out of packing crates. Some men had wives and children with them.

Instead of paying the bonus marchers, Hoover sent federal troops to remove them from their camp. The troops ended up setting fire to the camp and injuring many of the marchers. More than one hundred people died, including two babies.

As Franklin began traveling around the country campaigning, he could see the depression's effect on people. In many cities, homeless people had built temporary neighborhoods of flimsy shacks. People were calling these dismal places "Hoovervilles."

As bad as conditions were, Franklin "came home . . . with a conviction that the depression could be licked," Eleanor wrote. She admired his optimism and tried to put her own dread aside.

To help Franklin campaign against Hoover, Eleanor organized the Democratic Party's women in their own women's division—an unprecedented idea. Women had never handled campaign funds before. This year they did. In addition, a chairwoman in each state sent campaign plans directly to Eleanor. No candidate's wife had ever before had such significant responsibility.

Eleanor's women's division promptly rejected the promotional literature they were given and printed

Eleanor and Franklin during a campaign tour in 1932

their own "Rainbow Fliers." The fliers were so successful (the men started using them too) that they were eventually printed by the millions.

Election night found Eleanor and Franklin at the Biltmore Hotel in New York. Franklin stayed out of sight while Eleanor greeted the hundreds of supporters gathered in the ballroom. When the returns came in, voters showed that they had chosen "to meet things with open minds." They elected Franklin Delano Roosevelt—known to thousands as FDR—by an overwhelming majority. Clearly, the American people wanted FDR's New Deal.

Eleanor later described her feelings. "The turmoil in my heart and mind," she wrote, "was rather great." Regardless of her reaction, however, she had a new role to play. She was about to become the First Lady of the United States of America.

WALKING TO THE WHITE HOUSE

Franklin's inauguration was five weeks away when Eleanor traveled to Washington, D.C., to prepare for her family's move to the White House. One of Mrs. Hoover's secretaries offered to send an aide with a car to pick up Eleanor. Eleanor answered that she needed no aide and no car. She wanted to walk.

March 4, 1933—Inauguration Day—was as gray and cold as the mood of the country. Franklin had worked hard on his inaugural address (Eleanor and a reporter friend, Lorena Hickok, had critiqued it for him in the

Enthusiastic crowds greeted FDR and Eleanor on inauguration day in 1933.

wee hours the night before). Franklin reassured the troubled nation, saying, "The only thing we have to fear is fear itself."

Eleanor echoed his refusal to dwell on the negative. When reporters asked her if she would miss life in New York, she told them, "I've found that I never miss anything after it's gone. The present is enough to deal with."

The next day, Eleanor and her secretary, Malvina Thompson (known as "Tommy"), went over the White House "from basement to attic." Eleanor ran the elevator herself rather than wait for a doorman.

Determined to have everything ready, she also helped move furniture.

Two days after the inauguration, Eleanor held the first press conference ever held by the wife of a president. Lorena Hickok, who was the Associated Press's highest-paid reporter, advised her about how best to handle it. That day and at all the press conferences that followed, Eleanor invited only female reporters "to make it more comfortable to deal with subjects of interest primarily to women," as she explained.

As First Lady, Eleanor began a new daily routine. She and her housekeeper first planned menus and food quantities (not an easy job since the number of guests at a White House meal frequently changed at the last minute). Eleanor next informed the head usher about family plans and guests. Finally, Eleanor met with social secretary Edith Helm to consider what invitations she should accept, what receptions she should hold, and other responsibilities. Eleanor didn't think any of these meetings were very important, so she kept them quite short.

Over the next hundred days, Franklin and his advisers put together an amazing array of programs aimed at helping the United States out of the depression. The New Deal programs, included giving relief (food, shelter, and other aid). But many New Deal programs were aimed at providing jobs. Congress, desperate for any solution to the nation's sweeping problems, passed New Deal legislation with unprecedented speed.

Eleanor, meanwhile, was no longer teaching, and she missed this significant work. Hesitatingly, she asked Franklin if he would like her to take responsibility for looking over any of his mail. He told her no. His secretary, Missy LeHand, wouldn't want the interference. "I knew he was right . . . ," Eleanor wrote, "but it was a last effort to keep in close touch and to feel that I had a real job to do."

Not a woman to remain idle, Eleanor began writing a book called *It's Up to Women*. Published in November 1933, the book focused on the role of women in helping the nation come through the Depression.

Eleanor also began hosting her own radio show. Her friend Joseph Lash pointed out Eleanor's sympathetic style. She "made her listeners' interests and problems her own," he said. People all around the nation could listen to the show. One radio station dubbed Eleanor "First Lady of the Radio."

ROOSEVELT SENDS HIS WIFE

Shortly after Franklin's inauguration, Eleanor learned that the bonus marchers who had been treated so badly by Herbert Hoover planned to return to Washington. She asked Franklin to treat them well, and he did. With Louis Howe in charge of arrangements, the marchers were given food, medical help, and even dental care.

One day, Eleanor took Howe for a ride in her car. He suggested visiting the old army camp where the marchers were housed. Eleanor got out to take a look while Howe waited in the car. One man asked her name and what she wanted. When she announced who she was, the men asked her to say a few words. She talked about her canteen work during World War I and about her tour of the battlefields after the war had ended. She then led everyone in a World War I song. The men cheered her. One marcher pointed out a sharp contrast: "Hoover sent the army," he said. "Roosevelt sent his wife."

Eleanor presented a problem to the Secret Service because she refused to let them accompany her anywhere. In desperation, the head of the Secret Service demanded that she at least keep a revolver in her car. She agreed. She had one with her that summer, when she and Lorena Hickok took a trip through New England and into Canada just for fun.

Eleanor thought that Washington, D.C., should be a model for the nation's other cities. Instead, the city seemed to have the worst neighborhoods, hospitals, nursing homes, and jails anywhere. One day, Eleanor decided to drive herself through Washington's slums. She expected her drive to bring attention to what she called the "disease- and crime-ridden back streets," and it did. She also told Franklin of the problems she had seen, serving once again as his legs and eyes and ears.

In the autumn of 1933, Eleanor traveled to West Virginia to investigate conditions in the coal mines there.

Bloody strikes had taken place. Many mining families had been evicted from their homes, which the company owned, and were living in tents. Even where miners had not been evicted, living conditions were awful. Eleanor described the company houses as "scarcely fit for human habitation." Many children were malnourished and ill.

Eleanor donated earnings from her radio program to establish a children's clinic in West Virginia. She and wealthy businessman Bernard Baruch also started a school at Arthurdale, a homestead project in West Virginia. Based on Eleanor's report to Franklin, Congress created a new nationwide program, the Resettlement Administration, to help people find work, build homes, and grow their own food.

Some Congressmen attacked the resettlement projects as too costly. Eleanor counted the costs another way. "Many human beings who might have cost us thousands of dollars in tuberculosis sanitariums, insane asylums, and jails were restored to usefulness," she pointed out.

In the spring of 1934, Franklin suggested that Eleanor travel to Puerto Rico. He had heard reports that some sugar companies were paying people pitifully low wages and that embroidered linens made for export to the United States were being produced under terrible conditions. Eleanor found the reports to be true. She told American women to stop buying embroidered goods from Puerto Rico. She asked

Franklin to develop new, better-paying industries in Puerto Rico so that people would not go unemployed.

"Franklin, I Think You Should . . ."

Eleanor had become a highly visible advocate for America's most vulnerable people. As a result, she received thousands of letters—more than three hundred thousand during her first year as First Lady alone. Every letter received a reply from Eleanor or a staff person.

Sometimes Eleanor forwarded a letter to the government official who could best address the problem mentioned in the letter. Recipients often thought they were getting direct orders from the president and so quickly took action. Sometimes Eleanor walked into an agency herself to speed its response to a problem.

In 1935 Eleanor began writing a daily newspaper column she called "My Day." It described her ideas, travels, and life at the White House. Eleanor was not an elegant writer, but people were interested in her. Soon "My Day" was appearing in newspapers all across the country.

Eleanor also continued to hold press conferences. She didn't talk about politics, but stuck to social issues and topics such as nutritious menus. One reporter contrasted the president and the First Lady: "At the President's press conferences, all the world's a stage; at Mrs. Roosevelt's, all the world's a school."

By 1936 the United States seemed to be recovering

DEAR MRS. ROOSEVELT

During the Great Depression, many children and teenagers wrote to Eleanor Roosevelt for help. Many, like this letter writer, felt ashamed of being poor.

Eleanor addresses a crowd in Tennessee during the Great Depression.

Nov. 6, 1936

Dear Mrs. Roosevelt,

I am writing to you for some of your old soiled dresses if you have any. As I am a poor girl who has to stay out of school. On account of dresses & slips and a coat. I am in the seventh grade but I have to stay out of school because I have no books or clothes to ware. I am in need of dresses & slips and a coat very bad. If you have any soiled clothes that you don't want to ware I would be very glad to get them. But please do not let the news paper reporters get hold of this in any way and I will keep it from getting out here so there will be no one else to get hold of it. But do not let my name get out in the paper. I am thirteen years old.

Yours Truly,
Miss L. H.
Granette, Ark.

You can find this letter and others at an Internet site called Dear Mrs. Roosevelt. Go to the New Deal Network at <http://newdeal.feri.org/eleanor>.

from the depression. Franklin's New Deal had won the overwhelming support of American citizens. As he campaigned for reelection, he missed the help of his loyal friend Louis Howe, who had died on April 18, 1936. But Franklin not only won by a landslide (taking 60 percent of the popular vote) but also carried a Democratic majority into Congress.

In the spring of 1937, Eleanor set out across the country on a trip that included lectures and visits to "all kinds of places" where she could "get to know a good cross-section of people." She often showed up unannounced at government projects so "they could not be polished up for my inspection." And "of course," she wrote, "I always reported to Franklin upon my return."

The force of Eleanor's remarkable personality was felt by many who witnessed these reports. One observer recalled, "No one who ever saw Eleanor Roosevelt sit down facing her husband, and, holding his eye firmly, say to him, 'Franklin, I think you should . . .' will ever forget the experience."

*Eleanor was a remarkably outspoken First Lady. Here she casts
a vote in Hyde Park.*

Chapter SEVEN

DARNED BUSY

ELEANOR WOULD NOT COMMENT TO THE PRESS ABOUT politics, but she had a lot to say about controversial social issues. She often supported causes that Franklin could not support publicly for political reasons, but he never interfered with her activities.

One cause Eleanor wanted people to think about was racial equality. She spoke out against racism in many ways. In an article titled "What I Hope to Leave behind Me," she insisted that one "group of country-men cannot prosper while the others go down hill."

Eleanor wanted what she called "all-out support" for a bill against lynching—the act of executing a person without a fair trial. Lynchings were most often carried out by angry white mobs against African Americans.

Franklin refused when Eleanor asked him to back an antilynching bill. "First things first," he said. "I can't alienate certain votes I need . . . by pushing any measure that would entail a fight."

In 1938 Eleanor traveled to the Southern Conference for Human Welfare in Birmingham, Alabama. Accompanying her was African American educator Mary McLeod Bethune. When the two friends arrived, authorities told them that by law they were required to part. They must sit on separate sides of the auditorium reserved for blacks and whites. Eleanor captured public attention when she defiantly sat in the aisle between the two sections.

Another time, Eleanor confronted the Daughters of the American Revolution (DAR). Membership in this prestigious organization was limited to Americans who, like Eleanor, could trace their heritage to colonial times. The DAR refused to allow the famous African American singer Marian Anderson to perform at its auditorium, Constitution Hall, in Washington, D.C. In protest, Eleanor resigned her membership and arranged to have the concert moved to the steps of the Lincoln Memorial. Seventy-five thousand people attended.

Eleanor knew that her efforts on behalf of civil rights and other controversial causes created what she called "grave concern" among some of Franklin's supporters. They worried that Eleanor would hurt the president politically. When a reporter cautioned

Eleanor that some of her comments could get her into trouble, Eleanor answered, "What you don't understand is that perhaps I am making these statements on purpose to arouse controversy... and so get people to thinking about them." Franklin himself seemed undisturbed by anything Eleanor said or did.

Eleanor was also deeply troubled about the future of young people. She devoted considerable energy to the National Youth Administration (NYA), a New Deal program offering vocational (job) training to young people and helping them finish high school and college. Eleanor talked to Franklin about the program, pointing out that the leader of Nazi Germany, Adolf Hitler, had organized young people into youth groups that supported him. Eleanor worried that some Americans might compare the NYA to those Nazi groups.

Franklin was ready, this time, to ignore dissent. "If it is the right thing to do for the young people," he reassured Eleanor, "then it should be done. I guess we can stand the criticism." As it turned out, the NYA became politically popular and actually strengthened Franklin's presidency.

A TROUBLED WORLD

Beginning in the summer of 1938, a parade of European visitors were guests at the White House and Hyde Park. The Roosevelts entertained the king and queen of England and royalty from Sweden, Norway, and Denmark.

The leaders of European nations were reaching out to the United States for help. Tensions all around the world had been steadily mounting over the last several years. Japan had seized Manchuria in China in 1931 and attacked China again in 1937. Benito Mussolini had risen to power in Italy and invaded Ethiopia in 1935. General Francisco Franco had overthrown an elected government in Spain in 1936. And Germany, led by Adolf Hitler, seized control of Austria in 1938. Another world war seemed to be looming.

Most Americans, however, wanted the United States to remain isolated—separated from the problems of the rest of the world. American books and films portrayed World War I as futile. College students took pledges never to fight a similar war, and Congress passed a series of isolationist laws.

Franklin was acutely aware of the worsening situation and wanted American armed forces to be prepared to defend the United States. He also wanted the United States to support its allies, including Great Britain and France. With his encouragement, Congress did vote some funds to expand the navy.

In November 1938, German Nazis went on a wave of looting, arson, and cruelty against Jews in Germany. Anti-Nazi and Jewish groups in the United States wanted Congress to pass a bill allowing more German Jews, especially children, to flee to the United States. A Jewish judge asked Eleanor to support the bill, which she did, but it failed in Congress.

"What has happened to us in this country?" an indignant Eleanor wrote in her newspaper column. "We have always been ready to receive the unfortunates from other countries, and though this may seem a generous gesture on our part, we have profited a thousand fold by what they have brought us."

In July 1939, Franklin asked Congress to repeal a law against selling weapons to "belligerent nations" so that the United States could ship arms to Great Britain and France. Congress refused, however. Many members of Congress, like other Americans, still wanted no part in a European war. Franklin dreaded the moment when U.S. involvement could no longer be delayed.

On September 2, 1939, Eleanor made a startling announcement in her column. At five o'clock that morning, she wrote, Franklin had told her that Germany had invaded Poland. Outraged, Great Britain and France declared war on Germany on September 3. Franklin declared a state of national emergency so that he would have the power to act swiftly if necessary.

In March 1940, Italy and Germany joined forces against the Allies—Great Britain, France, Russia, and other nations. In April Germany invaded Norway and Denmark. On May 9, the American ambassador to Belgium called Franklin to say Hitler's army was attacking Belgium, Holland, Luxembourg, and France.

As the Germans destroyed the Belgian army, forced Holland to surrender, and overran Luxembourg and

France, even the most die-hard isolationists could see
that the United States was threatened. Congress finally authorized money to prepare for war. When Germany began bombing London and other British
targets, Eleanor lent her influence to help bring
British children to safety in the United States.

Franklin spent the summer of 1940 sweltering in
the Washington heat. Eleanor escaped to Val-Kill, a
fieldstone cottage Franklin had built at Hyde Park
for Eleanor and her friends Marian Dickerman and
Nancy Cook.

THE QUESTION OF A THIRD TERM

No U.S. president had ever served three terms. As Europe battled, Franklin's second term was drawing to a
close. It seemed to Eleanor that Franklin was looking
forward to retirement.

However, many people feared losing Franklin's
strong leadership, at such a troubled time. They
wanted him to consider an unprecedented third term.
"More and more people came to me saying that he
must run . . . , " Eleanor wrote. "No one else had the
prestige and the knowledge to carry on through a crisis."

Franklin eventually did run for a third term. In November he defeated his opponent, Wendell Willkie, by
almost five million votes. Plucky Eleanor had obvi-
ously forgotten the entries she had written in her
diary following Franklin's first nomination for president. "As usual," she crowed, "I wanted him to win."

Eleanor especially began to "feel that the war was close," as she put it, when her sons—James, Elliott, Franklin Jr., and John—began serving in the military. If the United States entered the war in Europe, the lives of Eleanor's sons would be threatened.

Life brought even more grief. On September 7, 1941, Sara died at Hyde Park. That same night, Eleanor's brother, Hall, was hospitalized for problems brought on by alcoholism. Eleanor spent the next weeks watching her brother suffer, until he died on September 25. For her, losing Hall was "like losing a child."

Whenever Eleanor's spirits fell, she immersed herself in work. "Work is always an antidote for depression," she wrote. She became cochair of the Office of Civilian Defense (OCD), which was helping civilians plan

Eleanor's sons Elliott, left, *and Franklin Jr.,* right. *All four Roosevelt sons served in the military during World War II.*

for the defense of the American home front. Franklin welcomed Eleanor's focus on the OCD. It meant she would leave him alone in other areas.

On December 7, 1941, at 1:40 P.M., Franklin was informed that Japan, an ally of the "Axis" powers—Germany and Italy—had bombed the U.S. naval base at Pearl Harbor in Hawaii. The surprise attack had killed more than 2,400 Americans and crippled the U.S. fleet in the South Pacific. Eleanor spoke to a shocked nation that night on the radio. "For months now the knowledge that something of this kind might happen has been hanging over our heads . . . ," she said. "That is all over now. . . . We know what we have to face and we know that we are ready to face it." The next day, the president asked Congress to declare war on Japan, and on December 11, Germany and Italy declared war on the United States. All-out war had begun among the Allied and Axis nations.

WORLD WAR II YEARS

The Japanese swiftly took the Philippines, Wake Island (an American possession), and Hong Kong. With American forces falling back in the Pacific, rumors began to spread that Japanese submarines would attack the West Coast of the United States. Eleanor flew there with Fiorello LaGuardia, mayor of New York City and cochair with her of the OCD, to calm people. When they checked on civil defense operations, they found the local governments basically unprepared.

The Japanese attack on Pearl Harbor on December 7, 1941, launched the United States into World War II.

Some people blamed Eleanor and, indirectly, the president. They charged them with "inefficiency, Communism, and do-goodism" in the OCD.

Eleanor had wanted to help the OCD. Instead she felt she was harming it because of these attacks. Eventually she resigned. "I realize how unwise it is," she said in a speech, "for a vulnerable person like myself to try a government job."

Eleanor began traveling around the country to visit her sons and other servicemen at bases where they were staying before being shipped to battles in the Pacific and in Europe. After the first moments of awe the men felt at seeing the First Lady, they enjoyed talking to her. She noticed men standing in long lines to get something to eat or drink. And in train stations, she saw servicemen sleeping on hard wooden benches. Eleanor contacted the Red Cross and the United Service Organizations to set up canteens and provide cots where needed.

In the fall of 1942, Eleanor went to Great Britain to observe the women's war effort there. Her old feelings of inadequacy crept in as she thought of visiting Buckingham Palace, but her fears were groundless. "The king and queen treated me with the greatest kindness," she wrote.

The queen showed Eleanor where the palace had been hit by a bomb and explained that the heavy curtains on the windows were for blackouts. Eleanor noted that residents of the palace ate nothing "not served in any of the war canteens."

Eleanor saw British women working at all sorts of jobs usually reserved for men at that time. When she visited the camps where American servicemen were stationed, she gathered the names and addresses of their families "so that I could write to them on my return to the United States," as she explained. "I had quite a collection before I was through."

Eleanor's trip was so successful that Franklin wanted her to travel to the South Pacific to meet the troops there. On the first day of her visit, she inspected three hospitals and an officer's rest home, reviewed a marine battalion, made a speech, and attended a dinner and reception. She continued that grueling schedule throughout her tour.

BACK AT THE WHITE HOUSE

In early 1944, Eleanor's daughter, Anna, and her little boy moved into the White House. Anna began taking over many of the duties of Franklin's personal secretary. Eleanor enjoyed having these family members with her. Anna, Eleanor wrote, "brought . . . a gaiety and buoyancy that made everybody feel happier because she was around."

Allied forces were advancing on both the European and Pacific fronts of the war. Victory seemed to be in sight as Franklin considered running for a fourth term. Throughout the winter of 1943 and 1944, he ran a constant low fever. Few people questioned, however, that he would run if his health permitted. Not surprisingly, Franklin did run and won the election by more than three and a half million votes.

After the election, Franklin went to Warm Springs to rest, along with two cousins, Laura Delano and Margaret Suckley. Lucy Mercer Rutherfurd joined them there. Lucy had become a widow (she had married Winthrop Rutherfurd in 1920, shortly after the discovery of her affair with Franklin).

Lucy and Franklin took afternoon drives, read by the fire, and dined together. Lucy, who had stayed in touch with Anna, wrote to Anna about a particularly pleasant picnic the two had shared. As Lucy described

THE QUOTABLE MRS. ROOSEVELT

I n Eleanor Roosevelt's many newspaper and magazine articles, books, and speeches, she made many "quotable" comments. Below are just a few of them:

"I have never regretted even my mistakes. They all added to my understanding of other human beings, and I came out in the end a more tolerant, understanding, and charitable person."

"I sometimes wonder whether the American public, which encourages the press to delve into the private lives of public servants and their families, realizes how much the family of a public man has to pay in lack of privacy for the fact that he is willing to serve his country in an elective or appointed office."

"With the new day comes new strength and new thoughts."

"The most important thing in any relationship is not what you get but what you give."

"I could never say in the morning, 'I have a headache and cannot do thus and so.' Headache or no headache, thus and so had to be done."

"The day of really working together has come . . . ," Eleanor told a gathering of African American educators.

"For me, as for almost everyone, I think, the things that mattered most have not been the big important things but the small personal things."

the way she listened as Franklin talked with her, Anna recalled, "I realized Mother was not capable of giving him this—just listening."

The family spent Christmas at Hyde Park. On Christmas Day, Franklin had a confidential talk with Elliott. He told Elliott how much he appreciated Eleanor, how much he respected her strength of character. Elliott reported Franklin's words this way: "'I think that Mother and I might be able to get together now... take some trips maybe, learn to know each other again. . . . I only wish she wasn't so darned busy,' he said. 'I could have her with me much more if she didn't have so many other engagements.'"

Franklin and Eleanor had thirteen grandchildren by this time, and Franklin wanted all of them to attend his fourth inauguration in January 1945. Because of the war, the day was subdued, with no marching bands or floats and few guests. Franklin gave a five-minute talk from the South Porch of the White House. He had lost weight and looked pale. His hands trembled as he spoke in the January cold.

Later that month, the president traveled to the Russian city of Yalta to meet with Josef Stalin and Winston Churchill, the leaders of the Soviet Union and Great Britain. They discussed postwar plans. One of Franklin's great hopes was that the Allies would form a new international organization—a United Nations (UN). The UN would replace the League of Nations, which had collapsed.

When Franklin returned, many members of Congress were shocked by his frail appearance. Eleanor was relieved when Franklin decided to relax at Warm Springs with Laura and Margaret.

Eleanor and Tommy, her longtime secretary, went to Hyde Park to open the house for the summer. Franklin called the next evening, and Eleanor sent him a long, chatty letter the next day. "You sounded cheerful for the first time last night, and I hope you'll weigh 170 lbs. when you return," she wrote.

Eleanor was attending a charity event the afternoon of April 12 when she got a telephone call from Steve Early, Franklin's press secretary. "He asked me to come home at once," Eleanor said. "I did not even ask why. I knew down in the heart that something dreadful had happened." She rode with clenched hands all the way to Washington.

At the White House, Steve Early told Eleanor the news. The president was dead. Again, Eleanor did not ask how or why. She called Vice President Harry S. Truman and asked him to come at once so that he could be sworn in as president. She cabled her sons. "Pa slipped away. He did his job to the end, as he would want you to do."

Eleanor then flew to Warm Springs. Finally, she asked what had happened. Laura told her that Franklin had been sitting for a portrait when he collapsed. Lucy Mercer Rutherford "was there as well," Laura said.

Eleanor went into Franklin's bedroom and shut the door. When she came out about five minutes later, her eyes were dry, and she sat down and asked some more questions. Laura explained that Franklin had seen Lucy at other times, both at Warm Springs and at the White House. Eleanor's daughter, Anna, had sometimes made the arrangements. Eleanor showed no emotion. She went back into the bedroom to choose Franklin's burial clothes.

The next day, Franklin's coffin was carried to the little train station in Warm Springs. The coffin was placed on a cradle in the rear car so it could be seen through the windows as the train made its way back to Washington. As darkness fell, all the cars except the president's were dimmed. "I lay in my berth all night with the window shade up ... ," Eleanor wrote, "watching the faces of the people at stations, even at the crossroads, who came to pay their last tribute all through the night."

At the White House, Eleanor asked that Franklin's coffin be opened. According to one observer, she "took a gold ring from her finger and tenderly placed it on the President's hand." After a simple service in the East Room, Franklin was buried at Hyde Park.

Eleanor and her Scottie dogs at Val-Kill

Chapter **EIGHT**

AFTER FRANKLIN

ELEANOR WAS SIXTY WHEN FRANKLIN DIED. THEY had been married for forty years, twelve of them in the White House. Eleanor felt her center was gone. In its place, she said, was "a big vacuum which nothing, not even the passage of years, would fill."

Eleanor moved to an apartment in New York with Tommy. Although Eleanor wasn't sure what she wanted to do, she knew what she did not want to do. "I did not want to run an elaborate household again," she said. "I did not want to cease trying to be useful in some way. I did not want to feel old."

World War II ended in Europe on May 8, 1945. Eleanor spoke on the radio, thanking the soldiers, war workers, and civilians who had made victory possible.

She urged Americans to go on to "win through to a permanent peace. That was the main objective that my husband fought for. That is the goal which we must never lose sight of." In August, when fighting ended in the Pacific and the Far East, President Truman himself called Eleanor to tell her that the war was over.

KNOWING HER DUTY

In December 1945, President Truman telephoned again. He wanted Eleanor to be one of five U.S. delegates to travel to London to help launch a new international organization. Franklin's dream of a United Nations was coming true.

At first Eleanor hesitated. She certainly wanted to do what she could to promote world peace, but she wondered whether she was qualified. She didn't have a background in foreign affairs. The United Nations was her husband's greatest legacy, she believed, and she didn't want to fail. Some members of Congress also doubted her and had urged Truman not to appoint her.

In January 1946, Eleanor did sail for London. She had committed herself, and she was ready to go to work. When she found a tall pile of paper in her stateroom, "I promptly sat down and began reading—or trying to read. It was . . . very hard work," she said. "I had great difficulty in staying awake, but I knew my duty when I saw it and read them all."

Another delegate on the ship asked Eleanor if she would be willing to serve on something he called "Committee Three." She had "no more idea than the man in the moon what Committee Three might be." Conscientious as always, Eleanor "kept my thoughts to myself and humbly agreed to serve where I was asked to serve."

As Eleanor learned more about Committee Three, she realized why she had been assigned to it. Committee Three dealt with humanitarian, educational, and cultural questions—the perfect place for an ex-First Lady with no experience in foreign affairs. Eleanor thought Committee Three "might be much more important than had been expected. And, in time, this proved to be true."

One of the most important questions that came up in Committee Three was what to do with the many people who had fled from their home countries during World War II. Many refugees did not want to return home, since new governments had taken power and might make them political prisoners. Delegates from many Eastern European countries, where Communists had seized power, wanted to require the refugees to go home. The United States and other Western countries disagreed, insisting that the refugees be guaranteed the right to choose. Eleanor capably expressed the U.S. position on this issue.

Eleanor proved to be an effective delegate and eventually won people's respect—even those who had doubted her. One delegate told her, "We did all we could to keep you off the United Nations delegation. . . . But now we feel we must acknowledge that we have worked with you gladly and found you good to work with."

In the spring of 1946, Eleanor joined the United Nations in a more permanent position, as the U.S. delegate to the General Assembly, the most powerful group within the United Nations. She became the chair of the Human Rights Commission. The chief task of this commission was to write an international bill of human rights.

Drafting the bill took several years, required a grueling schedule, and presented many difficulties because of the vast political, cultural, and economic differences among participating nations. For example, the United States thought every child should have a right to education through high school. Poor countries were struggling to provide even primary education for their children.

As philosophies clashed, so did personalities. At one session, the delegate from the Soviet Union, who had a habit of making long speeches attacking other nations, rose to speak just as the delegates were about to adjourn. "He seemed likely to go on forever, but I watched him closely until he had to pause for breath," Eleanor said. "Then I banged the gavel so hard that the other delegates jumped in surprise and, before he could continue, I got in a few words of my own.

Eleanor's work at the United Nations drew her into the international limelight.

'We are here ... to devise ways of safeguarding human rights,'" she told him. "'We are not here to attack each other's governments'. . . . I banged the gavel again. 'Meeting adjourned,'" she firmly declared.

In December 1948, the United Nations overwhelmingly accepted the Universal Declaration of Human Rights developed by Eleanor's commission.

TRAVELING FOR PEACE

Eleanor attended her last session of the UN General Assembly in 1952 after six years of capable service

Eleanor in Paris. She traveled relentlessly for the American Association for the United Nations (AAUN).

that had won respect for her around the world. She was not ready to stop being useful, however. She decided to work on behalf of the American Association for the United Nations (AAUN). The AAUN was trying to gain international support for the United Nations.

Eleanor was soon traveling on many missions for the AAUN. On one trip, she visited Lebanon, Syria, Palestine, Jordan, Israel, Pakistan, and India. She was "greatly impressed by what the Israelis had done to reclaim the desert." In Pakistan she met with the All Pakistan Women's Association. In India, Prime Minister Jawaharlal Nehru met her plane at the airport. Eleanor could not imagine that she was important enough for such special treatment.

The autumn of 1953 found Eleanor in Japan. After World War II, the United States had more or less imposed a democratic government in Japan, but "this

did not automatically change the old customs,"
Eleanor wrote. Japanese leaders hoped Eleanor
Roosevelt could explain democracy to their people.
"Everywhere the women were willing to talk . . . ,"
Eleanor found. "I think my being here has given the
women quite a lift."

Eleanor's good friend and doctor, David Gurewitsch,
joined her when she flew on to Yugoslavia for her first
visit to a communist country. They arrived during a
drenching rain. They decided to take advantage of the
empty streets to slip out incognito to find out what was
available in the shops and what prices were like. They
thought they had gone unnoticed, until they read a full
account of their adventure in the morning papers.

The AAUN hosted a huge fund-raiser in New York
for Eleanor's seventieth birthday. Many illustrious people attended. The party ended with a few remarks
from Eleanor. "I would like to see us take hold of ourselves, look at ourselves and cease being afraid," she
urged. Her final words were for her family, which had
grown to include nineteen grandchildren and four
great-grandchildren. More than any achievement, she
said, "I treasure the love of my children."

In 1956 Eleanor worked relentlessly in the campaign
of Adlai Stevenson, who was running for president. At
the Democratic National Convention, she secured the
nomination for Stevenson with a stirring speech. She
told the delegates it was "time for new beginnings."
Stevenson lost, however, to Dwight Eisenhower.

Eleanor had been writing her daily newspaper column since 1935. Her rigorous campaigning for Stevenson alienated some conservative newspapers such as the *New York World-Telegram*, which dropped the column. Others, such as the *New York Post*, were happy to pick it up.

In 1957 the *Post* sent Eleanor to the Soviet Union to write a series of articles about that country. As Eleanor toured with a guide assigned to her, she grew disturbed by the immense power the Soviet government had over its people. Everything, including homes and businesses, seemed to be owned by the government. The government assigned people to jobs and set their pay and determined who could travel. Newspapers, books, and magazines were censored. Anyone who spoke out against government policy risked imprisonment. Worst of all, it seemed to Eleanor that the Soviet people accepted this situation.

As part of her visit, Eleanor met with Premier Nikita Khrushchev. Their interview turned into a two-and-a-half-hour debate. When Khrushchev asked if he could tell the press that he and Eleanor had enjoyed a friendly discussion, Eleanor replied, "You can say that we had a friendly conversation but that we differ." She was happy to leave Moscow the following day.

Eleanor wrote an autobiography called *On My Own*, published in 1958. Although she was seventy-five, she was still looking ahead. "There is so much to do, so many engrossing challenges, so many

Eleanor with a copy of the United Nations Universal Declaration of Human Rights (in Spanish), 1949

THE UNIVERSAL DECLARATION OF HUMAN RIGHTS

The Universal Declaration of Human Rights outlines the "equal and inalienable rights of all members of the human family." Just a few of its articles follow.

Article 1
All human beings are born free and equal in dignity and rights. . . .

Article 2
Everyone is entitled to all the rights and freedoms set forth in this Declaration, without distinction of any kind, such as race, colour, sex, language, religion, political or other opinion, national or social origin, property, birth, or other status. . . .

Article 3
Everyone has the right to life, liberty, and security of person.

Article 4
No one shall be held in slavery or servitude. . . .

Article 5
No one shall be subjected to torture or to cruel, inhuman, or degrading treatment or punishment.

heartbreaking and pressing needs, so much in every day that is profoundly interesting," she wrote.

In addition to "My Day," which Eleanor had cut back to three days a week, she also wrote a question-and-answer page each month for *McCall's* magazine. In 1960 her book *You Learn by Living* was published. She hosted a television show called *Prospects of Mankind,* and she lectured at Brandeis University. She didn't want to be called "professor," though, because she thought she didn't deserve the title. Eleanor even agreed to do a television commercial for margarine because she could purchase CARE packages for needy people abroad with the thirty-five-thousand-dollar fee. "For that amount of money," she explained, "I can save six thousand lives."

Eleanor Roosevelt was America's "Most Admired Woman." She still hardly realized this, however. For example, when she arrived at the 1960 Democratic National Convention in Los Angeles, "people stood up and there was an ovation," according to her friend Joseph Lash. "She quickly took her seat and began fiddling with her purse. David Gurewitsch, her doctor and close friend, nudged her. 'It's for you. You have to get up.' Under protest she did, but sat down quickly. It was rude to interrupt the speaker on the platform, she said, and later wrote him an apology."

As Eleanor grew older, she periodically admitted that "I suppose I must slow down," and members of her family certainly thought so. But Eleanor believed that if you pay too much attention to the inevitable aches and pains, "the first thing you know you're an invalid."

President John F. Kennedy appointed Eleanor as a delegate to the Special Session of the UN General Assembly that convened in March 1961. When she entered the chamber, the delegates applauded her. Kennedy also asked Eleanor to preside over the Commission on the Status of Women. (She had sent him a three-page list of women to consider after she learned he had included only nine women in his first 240 appointments.) In 1962 she traveled to Europe for her *Prospects of Mankind* program and started thinking about doing a TV series on books.

To outsiders, Eleanor seemed as dynamic as ever, but she began to tire easily and doze off. David Gurewitsch diagnosed her with a blood disease called aplastic anemia. Eleanor was hospitalized. But she had little patience with the nurses who took her blood pressure and gave her injections of medicine. She recovered, but she was weak, often had difficulty breathing, and sometimes trembled.

Eleanor was hospitalized again in September. She left the hospital three weeks later but remained frail and confused. On November 7, 1962, she died. She was buried as she wished—next to Franklin in the rose garden at Hyde Park, in a plain wooden coffin softened by pine boughs from the woods.

EPILOGUE

Eleanor Roosevelt had never thought of herself as a gifted person. "I had really only three assets," she believed. "I was keenly interested, I accepted every challenge and every opportunity to learn more, and I had great energy and self-discipline." As a result, she said, she had "never had to look for interests to fill my life."

The sum of Eleanor Roosevelt's influence is incalculable. One observer wrote, "It would be impossible to

Eleanor in 1961 looked back on a lifetime of extraordinary achievement.

say. . . to what extent American governmental processes have been turned in new directions because of her determination. . . . The whole, if it could be totaled, would be formidable."

But Eleanor's influence extended far beyond "governmental processes." She encouraged a troubled America during the Great Depression and a catastrophic world war. She spoke out on important issues such as justice for all, regardless of race. She helped to knit together the diverse and often embattled nations of her time. She served as a new model for American women.

According to Eleanor's friend Adlai Stevenson, her achievements never grew out of a desire for her own recognition. The tasks Eleanor set for herself grew out of believing, as she put it, that "what one has to do usually can be done." With uncommon courage and energy, she "did what was worth doing," as Adlai Stevenson said. His was a worthy tribute to Eleanor, a remarkable American whose loftiest aspiration, after all, was to be useful.

SOURCES

9 Russell Freedman, *Eleanor Roosevelt: A Life of Discovery* (New York: Clarion Books, 1993), 136.

9 Joseph Lash, *Eleanor and Franklin* (New York: W. W. Norton & Company, 1971), 688.

9 Doris Kearns Goodwin, *No Ordinary Time: Franklin & Eleanor Roosevelt: The Home Front in World War II* (New York: Simon & Schuster, 1994), 464.

12 Lash, 14.

12 Eleanor Roosevelt, *The Autobiography of Eleanor Roosevelt* (New York: Da Capo Press, Inc., 1992), 5.

12 Blanche Wiesen Cook, *Eleanor Roosevelt: Volume 1, 1884–1933* (New York: Penguin Books, 1992), 46.

13 Roosevelt, 5, 3, 7.

14 Goodwin, 92.

14 Roosevelt, 5.

15 Lash, 31, 32.

16 Cook, 58.

16–17 Roosevelt, 9, 8, 12, 6.

18–19 Ibid., 6, 9, 10.

19–20 Lash, 61.

20–21 Roosevelt, 13.

22 Lash, 67.

26–29 Roosevelt, 23, 24, 27, 29.

28–30 Ibid., 29–31, 37.

32 Lash, 100.

33 Roosevelt, 41.

33 Freedman, 44.

35 Lash, 126, 139.

37 Roosevelt, 49.

38 Lash, 141.

38–39 Ibid., 55, 57.

40–41 Ibid., 59–60, 61, 62.

42–43 Ibid., 166, 274.

46–47 Ibid., 197, 207, 220.

49 Ibid., 218.

50   Roosevelt, 98.
50   Cook, 233.
50   Lash, 237.
51   Cook, 251.
51   Roosevelt, 104–105.
51   Lash, 240.
52   Roosevelt, 109.
52   Lash, 256.
53–54   Roosevelt, 110, 112, 113.
54   Lash, 244.
55–57   Ibid., 118, 119, 121, 124, 125.
58   Cook, 360.
59   Roosevelt, 146.
59   Cook, 381–382.
61   Roosevelt, 149.
62   Ibid., 154–155.
63   Cook, 430, 433.
64   Ibid., 423, 427.
64   Roosevelt, 161.
64   Lash, 349.
64   Roosevelt, 160, 163.
66   Ibid., 161–162.
67   Cook, 423.
67   Roosevelt, 163.
68   Lash, 354.
68   Roosevelt, 162, 164.
69–70   Lash, 361, 358, 419.
71   Ibid., 367.
71   Ibid., 366.
72   Roosevelt, 179, 180.
73   Lash, 363
75   Freedman, 101.
75   Ibid., 457–458.
77   Ibid., 382.
78   Roosevelt, 191–192.
79   Lash, 363, 540.
81   Ibid., 575.
82–83   Roosevelt, 214, 220, 224.
83   Goodwin, 280.

84–85   Lash, 646–647, 650, 652.
86–87   Roosevelt, 240, 241, 243, 264.
   89   Goodwin, 562.
   89   Ibid., 568.
   90   Ibid., 600.
   90   Roosevelt, 275–276.
   90   Goodwin, 604, 611.
   91   Roosevelt, 276.
   91   Goodwin, 613.
   93   Roosevelt, 283–284.
94–95   Joseph Lash, *Eleanor: The Years Alone* (New York:
        W. W. Norton & Co., 1972), 23.
94–95   Roosevelt, 300–301, 302, 303.
96–97   Ibid., 308, 315, 320.
98–99   Ibid., 327, 334.
99–100 Lash, 239, 256.
  100   Roosevelt, 383.
  102   Ibid., 439.
  102   Lash, 304, 295, 303.
102–103 Ibid., 295.
103–104 Roosevelt, 410, 439.
  104   Lash, 458.
  105   Roosevelt, 97.

SELECTED BIBLIOGRAPHY

Cook, Blanche Wiesen. *Eleanor Roosevelt: Volume 1, 1884–1933*.
    New York: Penguin Books, 1992.
_____. *Eleanor Roosevelt: Volume 2, 1933-1938*. New York:
    Viking, 1999.
Freedman, Russell. *Eleanor Roosevelt: A Life of Discovery*. New
    York: Clarion Books, 1993.
Goodwin, Doris Kearns. *No Ordinary Time: Franklin & Eleanor
    Roosevelt: The Home Front in World War II*. New York: Simon
    & Schuster, 1994.
Lash, Joseph. *Eleanor: The Years Alone*. New York: W. W. Norton
    & Co., 1972.

_____. *Eleanor and Franklin: The Story of Their Relationship Based on Eleanor's Private Papers.* New York: W. W. Norton & Co., 1971.

_____. *Life Was Meant to Be Lived: A Contemporary Portrait of Eleanor Roosevelt.* New York: W. W. Norton & Co., 1984.

Roosevelt, Eleanor. *The Autobiography of Eleanor Roosevelt.* New York: Da Capo Press, Inc., 1992 [Includes *This Is My Story, This I Remember, On My Own,* and *The Search for Understanding*].

_____. *My Days.* New York: Dodge, 1938.

INDEX

OTHER TITLES FROM LERNER AND A&E®:

Arthur Ashe
Bill Gates
Bruce Lee
Carl Sagan
Chief Crazy Horse
Christopher Reeve
George Lucas
Gloria Estefan
Jack London
Jacques Cousteau
Jesse Owens
Jesse Ventura
John Glenn
Legends of Dracula
Legends of Santa Claus

Louisa May Alcott
Madeleine Albright
Maya Angelou
Mohandas Gandhi
Mother Teresa
Nelson Mandela
Princess Diana
Queen Cleopatra
Queen Latifah
Rosie O'Donnell
Saint Joan of Arc
Wilma Rudolph
Women in Space
Women of the Wild West

ABOUT THE AUTHOR

Mary Winget is a long-time editor of award-winning nonfiction books for young readers. She holds an M.A. in English from the University of Minnesota and has written several books and magazine articles. A close observer of the national political scene, Winget works as both editor and writer to draw attention to the compelling human questions behind political personalities and endeavors, encouraging young people to participate creatively in our national political process.

PHOTO ACKNOWLEDGMENTS

Photographs used with permission of: Franklin D. Roosevelt Library, pp. 2, 6, 10, 13, 18, 24, 27, 31, 34, 36, 41, 45, 48, 56, 59, 60, 63, 66, 68, 74, 76, 83, 85, 92, 97, 98, 101, 104; Corbis/Bettmann-UPI, p. 88; W. Bryan Winget/Image Makers Photography, 112.

Front cover, back cover: Franklin D. Roosevelt Library.